SPREADING TH

WILLIAM CAXTON and T

Written by Charlotte Guillain
Illustrated by Jim Mitchell

Contents

Passing on ideas 2
What was life like when William Caxton was born? 4
Learning the trade 6
Discovering the printing press 8
Using the technology 10
Good business 12
Who is Tim Berners-Lee? 14
The world Tim grew up in 16
Tim's work 18
The World Wide Web 20
Sharing the Web 22
How the Web changed the world 24
What makes someone great at spreading the word? 26
How do we remember William Caxton and Tim Berners-Lee? 28
Glossary 29
Timeline 30

Collins

Passing on ideas

All through history, humans have invented things. We create new ideas and **technology** to help us in our everyday lives. Sometimes these inventions lead to huge changes.

William Caxton understood the importance of a machine that printed books. His actions made sure that many more people were able to read books and learn from them.

Tim Berners-Lee worked with a different technology, the **Internet**, and created the **World Wide Web**.

These two men lived hundreds of years apart, but they both changed the way we learn and how we communicate with each other.

William Caxton, born around 1422

Tim Berners-Lee, born 1955

What was life like when William Caxton was born?

William Caxton was born around 1422 in Kent, in the south-east of England. When he was growing up, most people in England worked on the land as **peasant** farmers. The land they lived on was owned by a few rich men. The peasants had to pay the rich men **rent** so they could farm and live on the land.

peasant farmers working on the land

Cities, such as London, were starting to grow at this time. People were **trading** with other countries and the wool trade in particular was making many towns rich.

At this time, only a third of the people living in England could read or write. Every book had to be copied out by hand, and it could take months or years for someone to copy out a single book. This meant there weren't many copies of books available for ordinary people to read.

Learning the trade

In 1438, William became an **apprentice** to a **merchant** in London. As an apprentice, he learnt all about how trade works. Then in 1441, he moved to Bruges in Belgium because it was a big centre of trade. Merchants from all over Europe went there to buy and sell goods, such as wool.

In Bruges, William became the leader of a group of English traders. This group was called the Merchant Adventurers in the Low Countries. His job was to get foreign leaders to agree to trade **treaties** that helped English merchants. He learnt to speak different languages at this time and **translated** French books into English, which was hard to do by hand.

This picture shows what Bruges looked like in the 1400s.

Discovering the printing press

Around 1471, William went on a trip to the city of Cologne in Germany and while he was there he saw an amazing new machine – the printing press! This machine could print books.

The printing press had been created by the German inventor, Johannes Gutenberg, between 1430 and 1440. He used a wooden press that people used to make cheese. Then he fitted letters on to the press that could be taken off and rearranged.

He also invented a special, oily ink that stuck to the letters and printed on to paper. With the letters on the press and using his ink, Gutenberg could **reproduce** a page of writing over and over again. To start with, Gutenberg and his staff could print about six pages a day. This was much faster than copying out books! Between 1453 and 1454, they printed 180 copies of the Bible.

Using the technology

William Caxton spent a lot of time learning about the printing press and understanding how it worked. Then he took the idea back to Bruges, because he knew how much time and effort this machine could save.

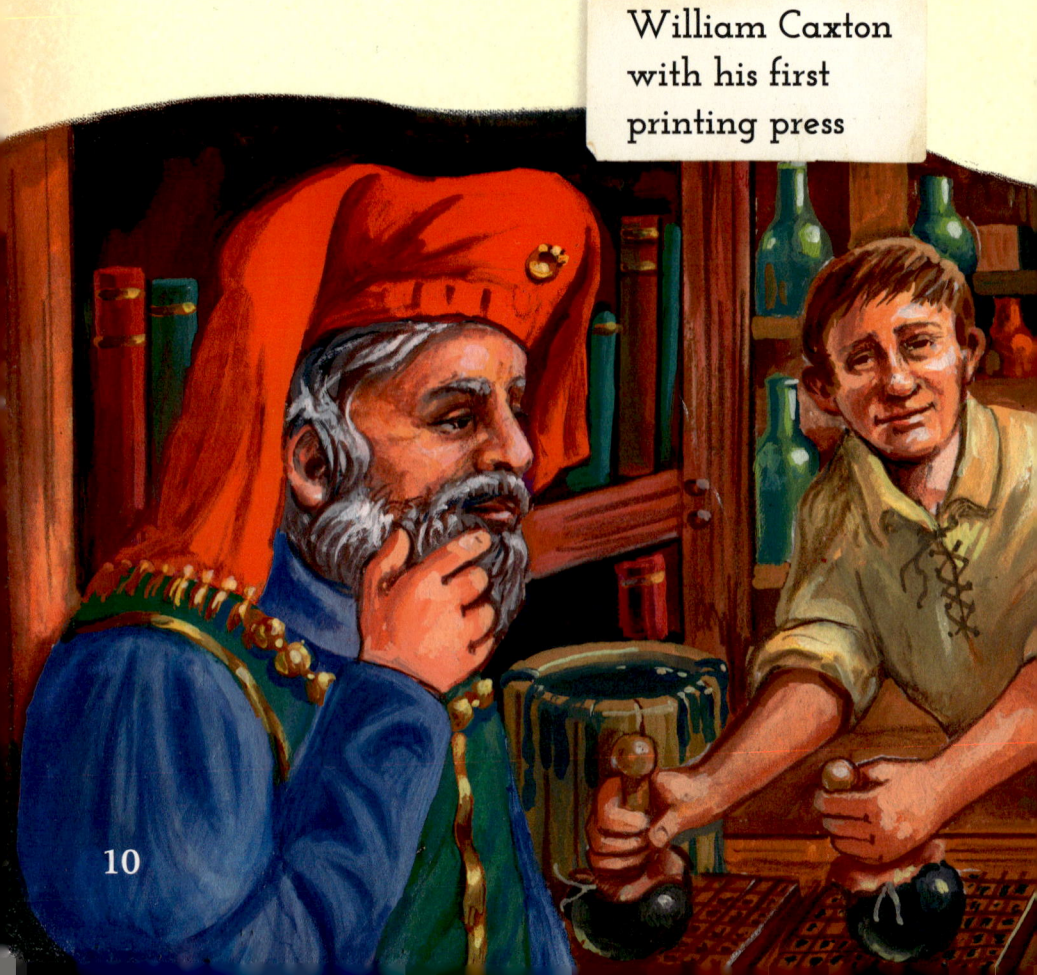

William Caxton with his first printing press

Around 1473, William printed the first book in the English language. Then, around 1475, he was the first person to bring a printing press to England. His press in London printed copies of more than 100 titles. William himself translated many of these books from other languages before they were printed in English. One of the most famous books he printed was Geoffrey Chaucer's *The Canterbury Tales*.

Good business

William Caxton understood that the printing press was a good way for him to make money. He knew that if he printed many copies of books, there would be more of them around for ordinary people to read. If more people learnt to read, then there would be more customers to buy his books!

He carefully chose to print books that he knew would be popular and sell well, such as *The Canterbury Tales* and stories about the saints and brave knights. This was good business for him, but it also made a big difference to people's lives. Before the printing press, only very rich people could afford to buy books. After printing arrived, people with less money suddenly had access to reading, and this made their lives better.

When he died in 1491, William Caxton had printed around 100 different titles. Before he brought the printing press to England, there were lots of different ways of spelling words and the English language was different all over the country. When many books were printed this helped to make written English the same everywhere.

Who is Tim Berners-Lee?

Tim Berners-Lee was born in England in 1955 and grew up in south-west London. His parents worked on one of the first computers that was developed for ordinary people to use. Tim was very interested in how things worked and took his model train to pieces to understand the **electronics**. Then he made his own electronic controls for the trains. He found this more fun than playing with the trains! He did well at school, especially at Maths, which his mother taught him from a young age.

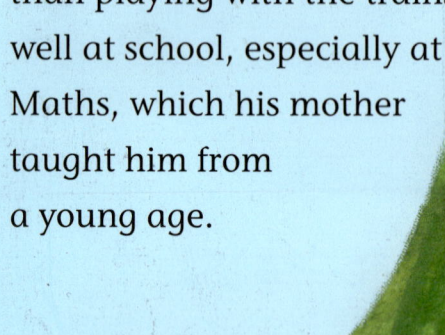

Tim Berners-Lee as a child

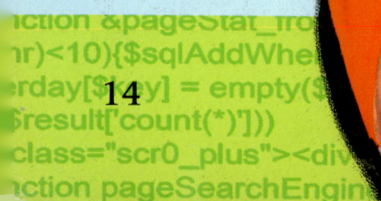

Early computers were very large!

15

The world Tim grew up in

When Tim was growing up, very few people used computers and the Internet didn't exist. People kept in touch with each other by speaking on the telephone but there were no mobile phones. A telephone was a large object that stayed in one place in people's houses.

old-fashioned telephone

People could also send letters and **telegrams** to each other, but it could take days to receive information.

machine used to send telegrams

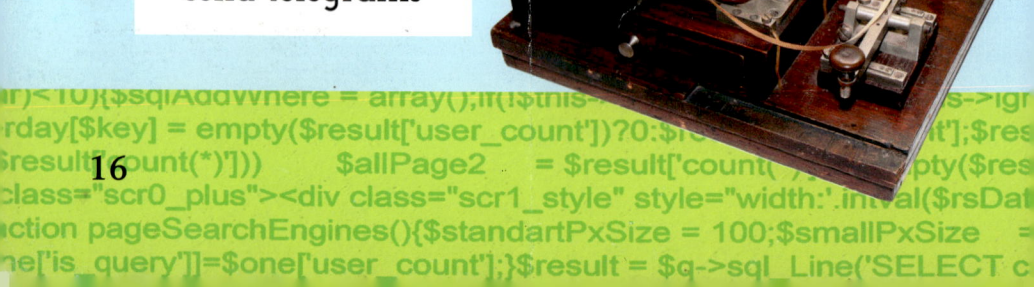

Anyone studying or doing research could only use books – they couldn't search on a computer.

The first email message was sent in 1971, but it was a long time before ordinary people started to send them.

Tim's work

Tim went to Oxford University in England to study Physics in 1973. He did very well in his studies and also built his own computer!

When he left university, he began designing **computer software**. Software is a collection of **programs** that give a computer instructions on how to do something.

Then in 1980, he moved to Geneva in Switzerland
to work in a large physics **laboratory**
called CERN. While he was there, he worked
on a computer program called Enquire.
This program let a person who was using
a computer keep information in files that
were linked to other files. It helped scientists
and researchers to share information. After this,
Tim started to develop ideas that would allow
people to share and access information
on the Internet.

The World Wide Web

Tim went on to invent the World Wide Web. He wanted people all around the world to be able to use the Internet to connect with each other and share their work and ideas.

The World Wide Web is what lets someone using a computer find information. When people look at websites, they are using the Web. It's made up of millions of pieces of information, such as words, pictures and videos, all grouped together.

To begin with, Tim thought the Web would just be useful for scientists. He thought they could use it to work on their research together and discuss and develop ideas more quickly. The World Wide Web was available for everyone to use in 1991.

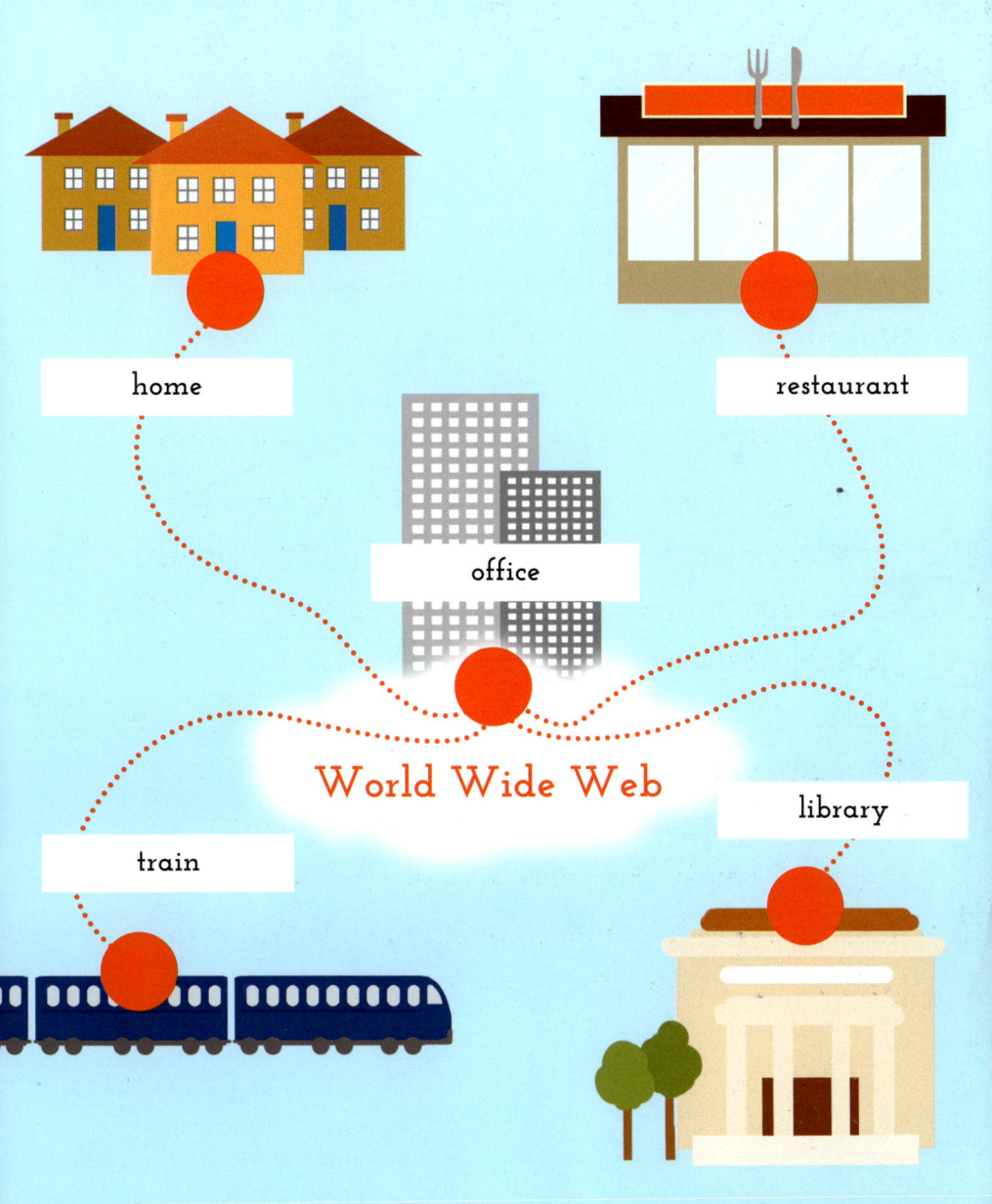

Sharing the Web

While Tim was working on his ideas for the World Wide Web at CERN, he was friends with a Belgian computer scientist called Robert Cailliau. In 1989, all Tim's time was taken up with his work on the Web but he needed money and support to help keep his work going. Robert Cailliau was very important because he helped to spread the word about Tim's work and he raised funds for it.

Tim Berners-Lee

After the Web was launched in 1991, Robert stayed interested in Tim's work. He helped to organise the first World Wide Web **conference** in 1994 at CERN. He also played a big part in helping to develop the way the Web was used in schools to help children learn.

the computers at CERN

Robert Cailliau

How the Web changed the world

The World Wide Web has made a huge difference to people all over the world. Before we had the Web, it could take a long time for people to get the information they needed. They had to search for what they wanted in libraries or they wrote to people requesting documents. People could send each other information, but it took time.

The World Wide Web changed everything. Now people can click from one website to another in seconds. People can work much more quickly and can spread and share information with other people all over the world. We use it in all parts of our lives. People learn and teach using the Web and they can also buy and sell on it. People can even meet each other and solve all kinds of problems using the World Wide Web.

What makes someone great at spreading the word?

William Caxton changed people's lives because:

- He made books available to more people in England, not just the rich.

- More books led to more people learning to read and getting an education.

- He helped to make the English language the same around the country.

Tim Berners-Lee changed people's lives because:

- He made the World Wide Web free and available to everyone in the world.

- He changed the way people work and communicate. Many things we do every day can happen very quickly because of the Web.

- People can get information easily using the Web. They no longer need to live near big libraries.

How do we remember William Caxton and Tim Berners-Lee?

William Caxton saw how important Gutenberg's invention was and by bringing the printing press to England, he changed the lives of millions of people through history. Printed books were the main way people shared ideas and improved their lives for centuries. He's remembered as someone who transformed the way we live using technology.

When Tim Berners-Lee invented the World Wide Web, he changed history again. Suddenly there was a new way for people to communicate and spread ideas. Just a few decades ago, ordinary people could never have imagined the Internet and World Wide Web or the gadgets we now use every day! Tim Berners-Lee will always be remembered as the man who had the imagination to change people's lives forever.

Glossary

apprentice — person who is learning to do a job

computer software — collection of programs that tell a computer what to do

conference — large meeting

electronics — to do with electrical circuits

Internet — global computer network that links millions of computers together

laboratory — building where people research and do experiments

merchant — person who buys and sells things

peasant — person who works on the land and is usually poor

programs — instructions for a computer to follow

rent — money paid to someone to use something

reproduce — make a copy of something

technology — creation of machines and inventions to solve problems

telegrams — messages sent electronically using a machine

trading — buying and selling things

translated — changed words into another language

treaties — agreements between countries

World Wide Web — a network of linked files stored on computers around the world

Timeline

William Caxton

Around 1422 — born in Kent, England

1438 — becomes a merchant's apprentice

1441 — moves to Bruges in Belgium

Around 1471 — sees printing presses in Cologne

1475 — brings the first printing press to England

1491 — dies

Tim Berners-Lee

1955

born in London, England

1973

goes to Oxford University to study Physics

1980

works at the CERN physics laboratory in Geneva, Switzerland

1991

launches the World Wide Web

Ideas for reading

Written by Clare Dowdall, PhD
Lecturer and Primary Literacy Consultant

Learning objectives: discussing the sequence of events in books and how items of information are related; being introduced to non-fiction books that are structured in different ways; answering and asking questions; explaining and discussing their understanding of books, poems and other material, both those that they listen to and those that they read for themselves

Curriculum links: History; Design and Technology; Computing

Interest words: apprentice, computer software, conference, electronics, internet, laboratory, merchant, peasant, programs, rent, reproduce, technology, trading, translated, treaties, telegrams, World Wide Web

Word count: 1,772

Resources: pens and paper/card, internet, video recording equipment

Getting started

This book can be read over two or more reading sessions.

- Read the front cover and the blurb together. Ask children to suggest what the title "Spreading the Word" means. Check that they understand that this is an information book about communication.

- Read the blurb again with the children. Ask them what their lives would be like without the World Wide Web. List examples of what they and their families use the World Wide Web for.

- Explain that this book is a dual biography about two people. Ask children to walk through the book to find out how it's structured (it begins with an introduction to both men, followed by a recount of each life in time order, and ends with a summary of both lives).

Reading and responding

- Read pp2–3 to the children. Develop comprehension and association by asking children to suggest some key technologies and inventions that are used in their everyday lives, e.g. light bulb, wheel, car, etc.